EVERYTHING
IS POSSIBLE

EVERYTHING IS POSSIBLE

Words of Heroism from Europe's Bravest Leader,

UKRAINIAN PRESIDENT VOLODYMYR ZELENSKY

— MARY WOOD —

SKYHORSE PUBLISHING
NEW YORK

Skyhorse Publishing books may be purchased in bulk at special discounts for sales promotion, corporate gifts, fund-raising, or educational purposes. Special editions can also be created to specifications. For details, contact the Special Sales Department, Skyhorse Publishing, 307 West 36th Street, 11th Floor, New York, NY 10018 or info@skyhorsepublishing.com.

Skyhorse® and Skyhorse Publishing® are registered trademarks of Skyhorse Publishing, Inc.®, a Delaware corporation.

Visit our website at www.skyhorsepublishing.com.

10 9 8 7 6 5 4 3 2 1

Library of Congress Cataloging-in-Publication Data is available on file.

Cover photograph by Future Publishing via Getty Images
Back cover photograph by Bloomberg via Getty Images

Print ISBN: 978-1-5107-7426-1
E-Book ISBN: 978-1-5107-7450-6

Printed in the United States of America

CONTENTS

A Leader Like No Other

SOME LEADERS TAKE POWER; OTHERS PROVE IT. When Ukraine elected President Volodymyr Zelensky in 2019 with an overwhelming majority, it didn't take long for critics to sound their skepticism. Surely a beloved actor and comedian didn't have the chops not only to govern a nation but also to defend three decades of Ukrainian independence and navigate a complex, post-Soviet conflict with such a foreboding aggressor as Vladimir Putin's Russia. But the people of Ukraine wanted a force for good who could fight for the democratic future befitting a modern European nation. They got this and more.

While President Zelensky had already begun his tenure as president of Ukraine emitting compassion, energy, and dedication to a more secure nation free of corruption, it wasn't until Vladimir Putin's Russian invasion on February 24, 2022, that the world knew what leadership looked like. In short order, President Zelensky became the reassuring face and gravelly, grounded voice that would invigorate his people to defend Ukrainian land, fight tooth and nail for Ukrainian values, and demand a Ukrainian future.

Stories flashed across screens everywhere: Of everyday citizens turned street fighters and aid workers overnight, of the unthinkable loss of loved ones and their way of life, and of heart-wrenching devastation as families became separated by bombs and borders. All the while, President Zelensky tirelessly and devotedly called his people and the world to action, not just to defend Ukraine but to protect the values of the world itself.

President Zelensky's fierce sense of duty and unwavering hope are reminders that values are to be cherished and defended, home is a shared identity, peace is indispensable, and hope is not a finite resource. On the pages of this book, this strength, sincerity, and stunning display of genuine leadership come through loud and clear. For President Volodymyr Zelensky, for the people of Ukraine, and for the future of the values that they hold dear: **EVERYTHING IS POSSIBLE.**

SERVANT OF THE PEOPLE

The president can't change the country on his own. But what can he do? HE CAN GIVE AN EXAMPLE.

—INTERVIEW WITH *THE GUARDIAN*

MARCH 7, 2020

Now it is true in the darkest time for our country, for the whole of Europe, I CALL ON YOU TO DO MORE.

—ADDRESS TO U.S. CONGRESS
MARCH 16, 2022

We immediately saw
that the world is truly
against the war.
TRULY FOR FREEDOM.
Truly for global
security. Truly for the
harmonious development
of every society.

—ADDRESS TO JAPANESE PARLIAMENT
MARCH 23, 2022

I really do not want my pictures in your offices, for the president is not an icon, an idol, or a portrait. HANG YOUR KIDS' PHOTOS INSTEAD, AND LOOK AT THEM EACH TIME YOU ARE MAKING A DECISION.

—INAUGURAL ADDRESS
MAY 20, 2019

I am almost
45 years old.
Today my age stopped
when the hearts of
more than 100 children
stopped beating.

—ADDRESS TO U.S. CONGRESS
MARCH 16, 2022

It's not me.
THIS IS ABOUT
THE PEOPLE
WHO ELECTED ME.

—INTERVIEW WITH *WORLD NEWS TONIGHT*
MARCH 7, 2022

We can do a lot together with you. EVEN MORE THAN WE CAN IMAGINE.

—ADDRESS TO JAPANESE PARLIAMENT
MARCH 23, 2022

I want to do
SOMETHING TO CHANGE
mistrust toward
politicians.

—INTERVIEW WITH *THE ECONOMIST*
MARCH 14, 2019

WE HAVE TO UNITE
in our energy.
We have to be united
because that means
that salvation is there.

—INTERVIEW WITH *FAREED ZAKARIA GPS*
MARCH 20, 2022

PEACE IS MORE IMPORTANT THAN INCOME,

and we have to defend this principle in the whole world.

—ADDRESS TO U.S. CONGRESS
MARCH 16, 2022

I do not try to play a role.
I feel good being myself
and saying what I think.

—INTERVIEW WITH *THE GUARDIAN*

MARCH 7, 2020

All my life I tried to
do all I could so that
Ukrainians laughed.
That was my mission.
NOW I WILL DO ALL I CAN
so that Ukrainians at least
do not cry anymore.

—INAUGURAL ADDRESS
MAY 20, 2019

I AM THE CITIZEN
of my country.
I am the elected president
of these people.

—INTERVIEW WITH *WORLD NEWS TONIGHT*

MARCH 7, 2022

I never wanted to be a country which is begging [for] something on its knees. **AND WE ARE NOT GOING TO BE THAT COUNTRY,** and I do not want to be that president.

—INTERVIEW WITH *WORLD NEWS TONIGHT*
MARCH 7, 2022

Let's find those people whose names do not cause controversy in our present and in our future.

—INTERVIEW WITH *THE TIMES OF ISRAEL*
JANUARY 19, 2020

We will build the country
of other opportunities—
the one WHERE ALL ARE
EQUAL BEFORE THE LAW
and where all the rules are
honest and transparent,
THE SAME FOR EVERYONE.

—INAUGURAL ADDRESS
MAY 20, 2019

Let's name the
monuments and streets
for those people
whose names do not
provoke conflict.

—INTERVIEW WITH *THE TIMES OF ISRAEL*
JANUARY 19, 2020

I see no sense in life
IF IT CANNOT
STOP THE DEATHS.
And this is my main issue
as the leader of my people,
GREAT UKRAINIANS.

—ADDRESS TO U.S. CONGRESS
MARCH 16, 2022

You can't think of the global and close your eyes to the details.

**—ADDRESS TO U.N. GENERAL ASSEMBLY
SEPTEMBER 25, 2019**

BELIEVE YOU ME,
EVERY SQUARE OF TODAY,
no matter what it's called,
IS GOING TO BE CALLED
FREEDOM SQUARE,
IN EVERY CITY
OF OUR COUNTRY.

—ADDRESS TO EUROPEAN PARLIAMENT
MARCH 1, 2022

I AM NOT
A POLITICIAN.
I am just a
simple person who
has come to
BREAK DOWN
this system.

—TO UKRAINIAN VOTERS
APRIL 2019

I can assure you that
I'M READY TO PAY
ANY PRICE
to stop the deaths
of our heroes.

—INAUGURAL ADDRESS
MAY 20, 2019

My position in life is to be a human being above all.

—INTERVIEW WITH *TIME*

DECEMBER 2, 2019

We have proven that
at a minimum,
we are exactly the
same as you are.
SO DO PROVE THAT
YOU ARE WITH US.
Do prove that you
will not let us go.

—ADDRESS TO EUROPEAN PARLIAMENT
MARCH 1, 2022

The more THIS BEAST will eat, he wants MORE, MORE, AND MORE.

—INTERVIEW WITH *WORLD NEWS TONIGHT*

MARCH 7, 2022

You cannot force people
to love the enemy.
WHAT YOU CAN DO
IS MAKE THEM PAUSE.

—INTERVIEW WITH *FAREED ZAKARIA GPS*

MARCH 20, 2022

THEY DEFINITELY HAVE EMPTINESS

instead of heart.

INSTEAD OF SOUL.

Instead of everything
that makes a
human, human.

—VIDEO ADDRESS
MARCH 22, 2022

I am just a common guy
from a common family
from a common industrial
town in Eastern Ukraine.
YET HERE I AM TODAY . . .
because EVERYTHING
IS POSSIBLE.

—ADDRESS AT STANFORD UNIVERSITY
SEPTEMBER 2, 2021

I was once asked:
why do you love Ukraine?
Strange question.
And why do you love
your mother?
SHE GAVE BIRTH TO YOU,
raised you, raised
you to your feet.

—ADDRESS ON THE ANNIVERSARY OF
UKRAINIAN INDEPENDENCE
AUGUST 24, 2019

We have similar
values with you despite
the huge distance
between our countries.
**A DISTANCE THAT
DOESN'T REALLY EXIST.**
Because we have
EQUALLY WARM HEARTS.

—ADDRESS TO JAPANESE PARLIAMENT

MARCH 23, 2022

SEE OUR FACES

YOU WILL SEE OUR FACES— NOT OUR BACKS, BUT OUR FACES.

—APPEAL TO RUSSIAN CITIZENS, KYIV, UKRAINE
FEBRUARY 22, 2022

I have the honor to greet you on behalf of the Ukrainian people, brave and freedom-loving people who for eight years have been resisting the Russian aggression, those who give their best sons and daughters to stop this full-scale Russian invasion.

—ADDRESS TO U.S. CONGRESS
MARCH 16, 2022

Only in peace.
ONLY IN DIGNITY.

—ADDRESS TO FRENCH PARLIAMENT
MARCH 23, 2022

NOBODY
is going to break us.

—ADDRESS TO EUROPEAN PARLIAMENT
MARCH 1, 2022

OUR PEOPLE have become this army.

—CONVERSATION WITH POPE FRANCIS
MARCH 22, 2022

PLEASE REMEMBER:
this is practical,
modern-day history
of Ukraine.
WE WANT TO LIVE.
We want to have peace.

—ADDRESS TO CANADIAN PARLIAMENT

MARCH 15, 2022

People throughout the planet have shared values.

—INTERVIEW WITH *FAREED ZAKARIA GPS*

MARCH 20, 2022

WE ARE STRONG.

—ADDRESS TO EUROPEAN PARLIAMENT
MARCH 1, 2022

WE MUST MOVE FORWARD,
build the country together,
do the impossible together
and say to ourselves every
morning "I AM UKRAINIAN.
AND I CAN DO ANYTHING!"

—ADDRESS ON THE ANNIVERSARY
OF UKRAINIAN INDEPENDENCE
AUGUST 24, 2019

Our people are
very much motivated.
VERY MUCH SO.
We are fighting for
our RIGHTS.
For our FREEDOMS.
For life. For OUR LIFE.
And now, we're fighting
for SURVIVAL.

—ADDRESS TO EUROPEAN PARLIAMENT
MARCH 1, 2022

EVERY MINUTE,
every hour, every day, the same things are happening:
PEOPLE ARE DYING.

—INTERVIEW WITH *WORLD NEWS TONIGHT*
MARCH 7, 2022

THE TERROR against us took place against children, against cities, and constant shelling has been taking place around the country, including hospitals, and that **DIDN'T BREAK US**, and that gave us feeling of big truth.

—ADDRESS TO U.K. PARLIAMENT

MARCH 8, 2022

But we are fighting also TO BE EQUAL members of Europe. I believe that today WE ARE SHOWING EVERYBODY THAT'S EXACTLY WHAT WE ARE.

—ADDRESS TO EUROPEAN PARLIAMENT

MARCH 1, 2022

On February 24,
**THE UKRAINIAN
PEOPLE UNITED.**
Today we have
no right or left.
We do not look at who
is in power and
who is in opposition.

—ADDRESS TO FRENCH PARLIAMENT
MARCH 23, 2022

Today the Ukrainian
people are defending
not only Ukraine,
**WE ARE FIGHTING FOR
THE VALUES OF EUROPE
AND THE WORLD,**
sacrificing our lives in
the name of the future.

—ADDRESS TO U.S. CONGRESS
MARCH 16, 2022

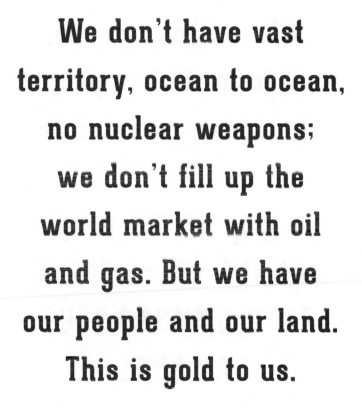

We don't have vast territory, ocean to ocean, no nuclear weapons; we don't fill up the world market with oil and gas. But we have our people and our land. This is gold to us.

—INSTAGRAM POST
MARCH 20, 2022

Who will suffer the most from it? The people. Who doesn't want it the most? **THE PEOPLE!** Who can stop it? The people. **BUT ARE THERE THOSE PEOPLE AMONG YOU? I AM SURE.**

—APPEAL TO RUSSIAN CITIZENS, KYIV, UKRAINE
FEBRUARY 22, 2022

I LOVE OUR LAND BECAUSE EVERY CORNER OF UKRAINE IS A BIG FAMILY.

—ADDRESS ON THE ANNIVERSARY
OF UKRAINIAN INDEPENDENCE
AUGUST 24, 2019

These ordinary people didn't have machine guns. **THIS COURAGE IS SOMETHING THAT IS UNPRECEDENTED,** and Russian soldiers don't even have that courage.

—INTERVIEW WITH *WORLD NEWS TONIGHT*
MARCH 7, 2022

The children and cities were being hit and hospitals as well with the rockets and constant shelling. **AND ON THAT DAY** we realized that **UKRAINIANS BECAME HEROES,** entire cities, children, adults.

—ADDRESS TO U.K. PARLIAMENT

MARCH 8, 2022

We do not have a "Ukrainian Dream" yet. But we have a "Ukrainian Goal" and a "Ukrainian Mission" to make THE FUTURE WE WANT FOR OUR COUNTRY.

—ADDRESS AT STANFORD UNIVERSITY
SEPTEMBER 2, 2021

YOU KNOW WHY THIS IS HAPPENING.

And you know
who is to blame.
Even those who hide
their heads in the sand
KNOW.

—ADDRESS TO FRENCH PARLIAMENT
MARCH 23, 2022

Many people look at us
and think that it will be
impossible to achieve
the goals we hope for.
BUT WE KNOW that our
critics are wrong.

—ADDRESS AT STANFORD UNIVERSITY
SEPTEMBER 2, 2021

And instead of
"Forgiveness,"
there will be a Day
of Judgment.
I'M SURE OF IT.

—ADDRESS ON FORGIVENESS SUNDAY
MARCH 6, 2022

The European Union is going to be STRONGER WITH US.

—ADDRESS TO EUROPEAN PARLIAMENT

MARCH 1, 2022

I LOVE UKRAINE

because I was born here.

I LOVE OUR FLAG

and I rejoice when it
flutters victoriously.

—ADDRESS ON THE ANNIVERSARY
OF UKRAINIAN INDEPENDENCE
AUGUST 24, 2019

I would never want
Ukraine to be a piece
on the map, on the
chessboard of big global
players, so that someone
could toss us around,
use us as cover, as
part of some bargain.

—INTERVIEW WITH *TIME*
DECEMBER 2, 2019

We're not asking for much. **WE'RE ASKING FOR JUSTICE,** for real support which will help us to prevail, to defend, **TO SAVE LIVES** all over the world.

—ADDRESS TO CANADIAN PARLIAMENT
MARCH 15, 2022

THE FIGHT
IS HERE

The fight is here;
I need ammunition,
NOT A RIDE.

—TWITTER POST
FEBRUARY 26, 2022

[Ukrainians] have not greeted Russian soldiers with a bunch of flowers. **THEY HAVE GREETED THEM WITH BRAVERY.** They have greeted them with weapons in their hands.

—INTERVIEW WITH *FAREED ZAKARIA GPS*
MARCH 20, 2022

I have a dream. . . . I can say, I have a need.
I NEED TO PROTECT our sky.
I need your decision, your help, which means exactly the same, the same you feel when you hear the words, **"I HAVE A DREAM."**

—ADDRESS TO U.S. CONGRESS
MARCH 16, 2022

All companies must remember once and for all that **VALUES ARE WORTH MORE THAN PROFIT.** Especially profit on blood.

—ADDRESS TO FRENCH PARLIAMENT
MARCH 23, 2022

I am sure that
Ukrainians are prepared
to stand against Russia
FOR THEIR ENTIRE LIVES.

—INTERVIEW WITH *WORLD NEWS TONIGHT*

MARCH 7, 2022

We are able to deal
a powerful blow.
We are able to strike back.
But unfortunately, our
dignity is not going to
preserve the lives.

—INTERVIEW WITH *FAREED ZAKARIA GPS*

MARCH 20, 2022

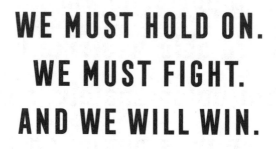

WE MUST HOLD ON.
WE MUST FIGHT.
AND WE WILL WIN.

—ADDRESS TO UKRAINE
MARCH 13, 2022

PROTECT EVERY METER

of our land and every
piece of our heart,
Ukrainian heart.

—INSTAGRAM POST
MARCH 14, 2022

WE WILL
fight until the end,
at sea,
in the air.

—ADDRESS TO U.K. PARLIAMENT
MARCH 8, 2022

INDIFFERENCE KILLS. Premeditation is often erroneous. And mediation can be between states, not between good and evil.

—ADDRESS TO ISRAELI KNESSET
MARCH 20, 2022

I am grateful
TO EVERY UKRAINIAN
and everyone who
stays around to
defend our cities,
OUR FREEDOM.

—ADDRESS ON FORGIVENESS SUNDAY
MARCH 6, 2022

SO TODAY I AM ADDRESSING YOU.

Honest, brave, rational and freedom-loving. . . . Because most of the puzzles that make up the answer ARE IN YOUR HANDS.

—ADDRESS TO FRENCH PARLIAMENT
MARCH 23, 2022

Eternal memory to everyone who died for Ukraine!

—INSTAGRAM POST
MARCH 15, 2022

Eternal curse
to the enemy who took
thousands of lives.

—INSTAGRAM POST
MARCH 15, 2022

Our weapon
is our truth,
and our truth is
that it's our land,
our country,
our children.
And we will defend
all of that.

—TWITTER POST
FEBRUARY 26, 2022

It's actually a war
against Ukrainian people.
AND IT'S AN ATTEMPT TO
DESTROY EVERYTHING
that we as Ukrainians do.

—ADDRESS TO CANADIAN PARLIAMENT
MARCH 15, 2022

Drive the occupiers out!

—INSTAGRAM POST

MARCH 21, 2022

Ukraine is the gateway to
Europe for Russian troops.
They want to break in.
BUT BARBARISM
MUST NOT PASS.

—ADDRESS TO ITALIAN CHAMBER OF DEPUTIES
MARCH 22, 2022

I think that all people
who came to our land,
all people who gave those
orders, all soldiers who
were shooting, **THEY ARE
ALL WAR CRIMINALS.**

—INTERVIEW WITH *WORLD NEWS TONIGHT*

MARCH 7, 2022

If we'll be attacked by
the [enemy] troops,
if they try to take our
country away from us,
our freedom, our lives,
the lives of our children,
WE WILL DEFEND
OURSELVES. Not attack,
but DEFEND OURSELVES.

—APPEAL TO RUSSIAN CITIZENS, KYIV, UKRAINE
FEBRUARY 22, 2022

When Russian forces demanded that we lay down arms . . . we did continue fighting, and **WE DID FEEL THE FORCE OF OUR PEOPLE** that opposed the occupants until the end.

—ADDRESS TO U.K. PARLIAMENT

MARCH 8, 2022

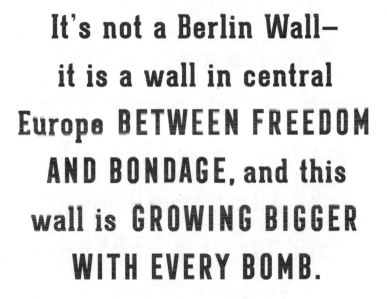

It's not a Berlin Wall—
it is a wall in central
Europe BETWEEN FREEDOM
AND BONDAGE, and this
wall is GROWING BIGGER
WITH EVERY BOMB.

—ADDRESS TO GERMAN BUNDESTAG
MARCH 17, 2022

IT'S ABOUT LIFE. . . .
Because every ruined family, every ruined house matters to us, BECAUSE WE ARE UKRAINIANS, and for us a PERSON IS PRICELESS.

—INSTAGRAM POST
MARCH 19, 2022

Ukrainians started protesting and stopping the armored vehicles WITH THEIR OWN HANDS.

—ADDRESS TO U.K. PARLIAMENT

MARCH 8, 2022

The [Ukrainian people] have not been looking to become big, **BUT THEY HAVE BECOME BIG** over the days of this war.

—ADDRESS TO U.K. PARLIAMENT

MARCH 8, 2022

The gap is closing, but the question is how long we can withstand [it].

—INTERVIEW WITH *WORLD NEWS TONIGHT*

MARCH 7, 2022

It's an attempt to
destroy our future,
TO DESTROY OUR NATION,
our character.

—ADDRESS TO CANADIAN PARLIAMENT
MARCH 15, 2022

We will continue fighting for our land, WHATEVER THE COST.

—ADDRESS TO U.K. PARLIAMENT

MARCH 8, 2022

WE ARE the country that [is] SAVING PEOPLE despite having to fight one of the biggest armies in the world.

—ADDRESS TO U.K. PARLIAMENT

MARCH 8, 2022

WE WILL NOT GIVE UP,
and we WILL NOT LOSE.

—ADDRESS TO U.K. PARLIAMENT
MARCH 8, 2022

If these attempts fail, then that would mean that this is a third world war.

—INTERVIEW WITH *FAREED ZAKARIA GPS*

MARCH 20, 2022

THIS IS THE PRICE OF FREEDOM. We're fighting just for our land and for our freedom.

—ADDRESS TO EUROPEAN PARLIAMENT
MARCH 1, 2022

STRONG
DOESN'T
MEAN BIG

STRONG DOESN'T MEAN BIG.

—ADDRESS TO U.S. CONGRESS
MARCH 16, 2022

I'm happy that we have unified today, **ALL OF YOU**, all the countries of the European Union.

—ADDRESS TO EUROPEAN PARLIAMENT
MARCH 1, 2022

Peace in your country
doesn't depend
anymore only on you
and your people.
IT DEPENDS ON THOSE
NEXT TO YOU,
on those who are strong.

—ADDRESS TO U.S. CONGRESS
MARCH 16, 2022

I think Ukrainians
are protecting the
values of ALL PEOPLE
who enjoy their lives.

—INTERVIEW WITH *WORLD NEWS TONIGHT*

MARCH 7, 2022

TRUTH WAS NOT FOUND IN THE OFFICES.

So now we have to look for it and gain it

ON THE BATTLEFIELD.

—ADDRESS TO FRENCH PARLIAMENT

MARCH 23, 2022

The world will not stop defending the truth. OUR TRUTH.

—ADDRESS TO G7, NATO, AND EU SUMMITS
MARCH 23, 2022

Perhaps this is
THE LAST CHANCE
for humanity
TO STOP WARS.

—INSTAGRAM POST
MARCH 19, 2022

YOU AND I MUST
NOT FORGET
that independence
did not appear
at the flick of a
magic wand.

**—ADDRESS ON THE ANNIVERSARY
OF UKRAINIAN INDEPENDENCE
AUGUST 24, 2019**

Everyone who is with us
will receive gratitude.
Not only ours, but also of
other nations of the world.

—INSTAGRAM POST

MARCH 15, 2022

People don't really
believe in words.
Or rather, people
believe in words only
for a stretch of time.
THEN THEY START TO
LOOK FOR ACTION.

—INTERVIEW WITH *THE GUARDIAN*
MARCH 7, 2020

Everyone thinks that we are far away. . . . No, when the limits of rising **FREEDOMS ARE BEING VIOLATED** and stepped on, then you have to protect us because we will come first; **YOU WILL COME SECOND.**

—INTERVIEW WITH *WORLD NEWS TONIGHT*

MARCH 7, 2022

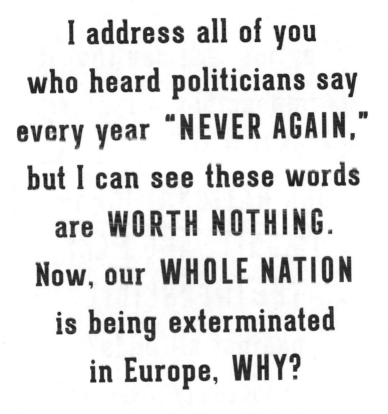

I address all of you
who heard politicians say
every year "NEVER AGAIN,"
but I can see these words
are WORTH NOTHING.
Now, our WHOLE NATION
is being exterminated
in Europe, WHY?

—ADDRESS TO GERMAN BUNDESTAG
MARCH 17, 2022

Skeptics will say that it
is impossible, a fantasy.
But what if this is, in fact,
**OUR NATIONAL IDEA—
TO UNITE AND MAKE
THE IMPOSSIBLE**
against all odds?

—INAUGURAL ADDRESS
MAY 20, 2019

Sips of fresh air will
definitely not help
anymore. It makes sense
to ACT TOGETHER.
To put PRESSURE
together. To FORCE
Russia to SEEK PEACE.

—ADDRESS TO FRENCH PARLIAMENT

MARCH 23, 2022

We have similar values with you despite the huge distance between our countries. **A DISTANCE THAT DOESN'T REALLY EXIST.** Because we have **EQUALLY WARM HEARTS.**

—ADDRESS TO JAPANESE PARLIAMENT
MARCH 23, 2022.

STRONG IS BRAVE and READY TO FIGHT for the life of his citizens and citizens of the world. FOR HUMAN RIGHTS, for freedom, for the right to live decently, and to die when your time comes, and not when it's wanted by someone else, by your neighbor.

—ADDRESS TO U.S. CONGRESS
MARCH 16, 2022

We are protecting the values that are shared by everyone, **NO MATTER WHAT LANGUAGE YOU SPEAK** or where you live. If you allow the Russian army to destroy these values, this will be the end, because Ukrainians are bearing those values.

—INTERVIEW WITH *WORLD NEWS TONIGHT*
MARCH 7, 2022

Today it's **NOT ENOUGH to be THE LEADER OF THE NATION.** Today it takes to be **THE LEADER OF THE WORLD.**

—ADDRESS TO U.S. CONGRESS
MARCH 16, 2022

Forcibly you CANNOT make yourself a friend.

—INTERVIEW WITH *FAREED ZAKARIA GPS*
MARCH 20, 2022

Being the leader of the
world means to be
THE LEADER OF PEACE.

—ADDRESS TO U.S. CONGRESS
MARCH 16, 2022

WE HAVE PROVEN OUR STRENGTH.

—ADDRESS TO EUROPEAN PARLIAMENT

MARCH 1, 2022

We remain humane even on day four of this terrible war.

—ADDRESS TO U.K. PARLIAMENT
MARCH 8, 2022

If there is just one-percent chance for us to stop this war, I THINK THAT WE NEED TO TAKE THIS CHANCE.

—INTERVIEW WITH *FAREED ZAKARIA GPS*

MARCH 20, 2022

It is **UKRAINIAN PEOPLE**
who are going through
this test . . . because
all of our people [are]
**THE ARMY OF EUROPE
RIGHT NOW.**

—INTERVIEW WITH *WORLD NEWS TONIGHT*
MARCH 7, 2022

It is now being decided whether all the aggressors on the planet—explicit and potential—will be convinced that the war they have waged will lead to a punishment so powerful that they should not start a war. That they should not destroy the world.

—ADDRESS TO JAPANESE PARLIAMENT

MARCH 23, 2022

[Germany] is a country that brought to Europe the wall. What is behind this wall? . . . This looks like politics to many, but THESE ARE THE STONES for the new wall.

—ADDRESS TO GERMAN BUNDESTAG
MARCH 17, 2022

Now we have a chance. A chance to show not only Russia, but also any aggressor, any terrorist-country, that the war will destroy not the victim, but the one who started it.

—INSTAGRAM POST
MARCH 19, 2022

UKRAINIANS
ARE INCREDIBLE.

—ADDRESS TO EUROPEAN PARLIAMENT

MARCH 1, 2022

GLORY TO
UKRAINE

I can say, as a citizen
of Ukraine, to all countries
of the post-Soviet
Union: Look at us—
EVERYTHING IS POSSIBLE.

—ADDRESS TO UKRAINIAN VOTERS
APRIL 21, 2019

Yes, Ukraine was beautiful, but now it will become great. Great Ukraine.

—INSTAGRAM POST

MARCH 20, 2022

It's a victory when the weapons fall silent AND PEOPLE SPEAK UP.

—INTERVIEW WITH *TIME*

DECEMBER 2, 2019

RIGHT NOW,

the destiny of our country
is being decided,
the destiny of our people,
whether Ukrainians will
be free, whether they
will be able to preserve
their democracy.

—ADDRESS TO U.S. CONGRESS
MARCH 16, 2022

The question for us now is to be or not to be. Oh no, this Shakespearean question . . . I can give you a DEFINITIVE ANSWER.

—ADDRESS TO U.K. PARLIAMENT

MARCH 8, 2022

IT'S DEFINITELY YES, TO BE.

—ADDRESS TO U.K. PARLIAMENT

MARCH 8, 2022

The desire for independence is embedded in our genetic code.

—ADDRESS ON THE ANNIVERSARY
OF UKRAINIAN INDEPENDENCE
AUGUST 24, 2019

If you see, and if you understand how we feel . . . how we fight against all the enemies for our freedom, SUPPORT US. SUPPORT US. And not only with words, with concrete direct steps. . . . And I think we'll win, of course together with all the world.

—INTERVIEW WITH *WORLD NEWS TONIGHT*
MARCH 7, 2022

The people of our country love democracy and freedom and will not let threats take those things away. **WE KNOW THAT ANYTHING IS POSSIBLE.**

—ADDRESS AT STANFORD UNIVERSITY
SEPTEMBER 2, 2021

Our land is unique, charming, **UNBREAKABLE**, incredible, amazing, fabulous, wonderful, beautiful. If it were not for our **MOTHERLAND**, humanity might not know these words. After all, they were all invented to describe Ukraine.

—ADDRESS ON THE ANNIVERSARY
OF UKRAINIAN INDEPENDENCE
AUGUST 24, 2019

IF WE WILL FALL, YOU WILL FALL.

—ADDRESS TO EUROPE

MARCH 5, 2022

If we win, and I'm sure we will win, **THIS WILL BE THE VICTORY OF THE WHOLE DEMOCRATIC WORLD**, this will be the victory of our freedom, this will be **THE VICTORY OF LIGHT OVER DARKNESS**, of freedom over slavery.

—ADDRESS TO EUROPE

MARCH 5, 2022

When we have so
complicated a history,
let's build a
common history.

—INTERVIEW WITH *THE TIMES OF ISRAEL*
MARCH 16, 2022

We want to be victorious.
WE WANT TO PREVAIL
for the sake of life.

—ADDRESS TO CANADIAN PARLIAMENT
MARCH 15, 2022

So, what now?
What do we have left?
OUR VALUES. UNITY.
And the determination
to defend our freedom.
Common freedom!

—ADDRESS TO FRENCH PARLIAMENT
MARCH 23, 2022

If we win, we will become as blossoming as Europe. And Europe will be flourishing more than ever.

—ADDRESS TO EUROPE

MARCH 5, 2022

Our capitals are separated. . . . But what is the distance between our feelings of freedom? Between our desires to live? Between our aspirations for peace?

—ADDRESS TO JAPANESE PARLIAMENT
MARCH 23, 2022

NO ONE

will give away

our independence.

—INTERVIEW WITH *WORLD NEWS TONIGHT*

MARCH 7, 2022

[Ukraine] doesn't give up, and we HAVE NOT EVEN THOUGHT ABOUT IT for a second.

—ADDRESS TO U.S. CONGRESS
MARCH 16, 2022

I'm sure you understand this feeling. This need.
THE NEED TO RETURN TO YOUR LAND.

—ADDRESS TO JAPANESE PARLIAMENT

MARCH 23, 2022

I'm confident that TOGETHER WE WILL OVERCOME and will be victorious.

—ADDRESS TO CANADIAN PARLIAMENT
MARCH 15, 2022

I beg you—do not stop.
Don't stop helping Ukraine.

—INSTAGRAM POST
MARCH 15, 2022

I would like the end to be like the Hollywood movies—the happy end.

—INTERVIEW WITH *WORLD NEWS TONIGHT*

MARCH 7, 2022

We do not want
to lose what we have,
what is ours, our
country Ukraine.

—ADDRESS TO U.K. PARLIAMENT
MARCH 8, 2022

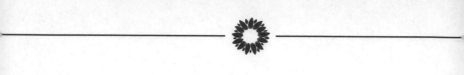

We will win . . .

There will be
new cities . . .

There will be
new dreams . . .

There will be

a new story...

There will be,
there's no doubt . . .

And those we've lost
will be remembered . . .

And we will sing
again, and we will
celebrate anew . . .

—INSTAGRAM POST
MARCH 20, 2022

GLORY TO UKRAINE.

—ADDRESS TO CANADIAN PARLIAMENT
MARCH 15, 2022

ABOUT THE AUTHOR

MARY WOOD is a writer, political researcher, and mother of two curious boys. She lives in northern New Jersey.